DIODE EDITIONS

Go because I love you

POEMS BY

Jared Harél

Winner of the Diode Editions Book Award

ISBN: 978-1-939728-20-3
Diode Editions
Doha, Qatar

Design & layout: Law Alsobrook
Author photo: Ilan Harel
Ordering & Contact information: http://www.diodeeditions.com

Contents

1.

2.

3.

Acknowlededgments

For Yael, Neta & Oren

1.

Go So You Can Come Back

Go so you can come back
says my wife, meaning go but don't linger
in frozen foods, or forget
where you parked, or chat up the cashier.
Go, certainly, because something
needs getting while the baby takes a nap,
and the snow isn't snowing,
and here are some coupons that happen
to be expiring, so go
before all the ripe produce
turns soft and stringy, and school lets out,
and a tallish boy hawking Skittles
by the entrance wins you over, and you throw him
cash, your wallet, everything for the sake
of his under-funded football team
because though you never loved football,
you love James Wright's poem about football
and solitude and those suicidally-
beautiful, galloping sons who go at it and go
because I love you, though I also love
those parmesan Popchips,
and to love is to leave
room for longing, but come back
so that we might go out together, later,
in a perpetual rotation of goings and comings
which requires nothing but patience
and faith that when we go
we remember where is home.

All Possible Fates

The universe is expanding, but my apartment
is not. This is balance I tell myself,
tripping over trikes, toy blocks,
the way a housecat can convince itself a mattress
is wilderness, its very own Savannah,
or how no one in the neighborhood can afford
the neighborhood, though we ghost
past townhouses, pretending they are ours.
In the end, isn't it in our nature to disperse?
To pull away? When my daughter begs to play
hide-and-seek, I try my best not to find her
immediately, though there are only so many places
to hide. Then one day, sick of ducking
behind sofa cushions, or under the desk, she slips
into the bathroom, snaps down the lock.
Three years old and well out of reach.
Before I knew I too could disappear, I would leap
off balconies, bunk beds and swings, bike
to the brink of each dead-end street.
I write this beside a man weeping into the *Arts*
& Leisure section of the Times. His lips
are quivering, face wet, yet what can I do but look
away? I look away, but he's in this now,
fixed inside, like how my daughter was a door
I threatened and pleaded with, until she felt
like having pancakes, and turned the knob. I admit
all fault, to all possible fates. Are we bound
to be an airport where everyone leaves?

My Years in Tacoma, Without Exaggeration

I hitchhiked to Boulder
on a hunch and three beers.

Each road I took, I took
for granted. Each town a postcard
I never sent.

Motion broke me
like a fly in amber.
That nothing came of it
proves nothing.

I lived on a shoestring, off
the books, forged kin-
ships I could split
in a blink.

A planet, I grew
to be measured from afar,

and the S sparked out
on that highway *SHELL* sign,
but if ever I was lost,
I'd trust it like a star.

New View

What luck the sunset is something to look at—
angelic grand gesture, braggadocio
of sky. Jogger in pink socks down a tie-dye avenue.

This high up, I show it to my daughter.
I say the sun's going to bed, and the colors
are its pajamas. I say this crap, and it becomes

her *childhood*, the deep, impossible
knotting of her heart. It's hopeless, I can't help
but speak of her heart: crimson motor of meat

and stardust. Little metaphor. Mighty
tug boat. I say, you know not everything I tell you
is true. She says the sun waves goodbye,
but the moon doesn't want to.

Those of Us Who Cannot Recall Our Dreams

What we rise from is nothing
to riddle our therapists,
or recount to lovers
in the aquarium of our beds.
There are no Minotaurs
joining us for supper.
No grim or gripping visitations
from the grave. Our lives
are light-switches
hidden in dark rooms,
but the other night, I caught
my wife uppercut
the comforter, adamant
that whatever it was
was hers. I have peeked
inside the bullet-hole
of her sleeping mouth and found
not a note. Not even the bones
of our life together.
She tows this hidden world,
ropes it to her waist
the way my mother once
leashed me to her wrist
in Magic Kingdom
so no one would take me,
and so I'd never escape.

Legion

Thebes fell. The Assyrians fell. The pills I swallowed
fell into my lap, making the white bathroom tiles
glisten and sing. Then my eyes rolled inwards
like the underside of a glacier, and I shook
in the Corinthian columns of my bones.

At the hospital, mulberries bloodied my one good window.
Still I could see a billboard for affordable condos
and behind it, the blue legion of sky.

Local News

Terrified we'd die happy and rich,
reclined at the lip of our shorefront properties,
we swiped a broad-axe from your dad's tool shed
and swore we'd seen a murderer or bear
stalking the dark coil of woods
behind our school. That's how desperate
we felt those days, how certain
we were there was nothing to see. You were the leader:
thirteen and over six feet. I was thirteen
but looked about seven, with parents who dreaded
those gothic letters thread into our hoodies.
Who could blame us for plugging our ears, tuning
them out? Still we craved being real
enough to vanish without a trace, our dour faces bound
to lamp posts, aged by a spot
on the local news. We fled that night with blades
and flashlights, fluorescent beams
slicing the trees. *What's that?* you whispered,
and whirled your axe towards a rabbit or squirrel.
What's that? we kept asking, our voices
rising, as if either of us could imagine
the answer to what we saw.

Veterans Day, 2014

Lately, I've been praying
for life to surprise me
like a pitch-black living room
primed to fracture
into song and streamers,
a hand on my shoulder
yelling, *Didn't think
we remembered, did ya?*
Lately, my counter-thoughts
have been riddled with guilt,
the way a stray wallet
excites before shaming,
though shame lasts
and bitters the tongue.
I saw coverage yesterday
of a third beheading
while doing crunches
on an exercise ball.
The ball, I remember,
was clown-nose red,
and never before had I felt
so damaged, so lucky
and absurd. I drove home
drowning in the hum
of sports radio, grateful
for the scores and in-depth
analysis. Someone
had become a restricted
free-agent. Someone
had been traded and was
finally coming home.

First Witness

The *you* you know
begins to give:

a potter's curve
at the base

of your abdomen, hips
upon which

nothing fits. And though
I cannot change

with you, I rise
from sleep

to pull you near:
a new you,

this evidence
of *we*,

which for these first
few months,

no one
but us can see.

Senior Cut Day

An act of defiance: I decided to show up,
attend every class, even take notes
though you couldn't do much with three or four students,
either Brian Hoffer with his coded binder
and early-admissions letter to Brown,
or Megan Dennis, recluse cellist, one absence shy
of being held back. While my friends played hooky,
drove to Jones Beach with Frisbees
and six-packs, expired sunblock
and disposable cameras, I stayed and ate lunch
with sophomores, let them in on my own private joke.
It was 1999. The Rapture at hand.
Our President was talking blowjobs
on C-SPAN. Getting high that night
in the bowling-alley parking lot, I heard Andre
pantsed Erin, how Goth Jimmy stripped
to swim, so pale he blinded the beach.
Marilyn Manson seared our ears, our '86 Mazdas
and rusted Fords. I could feel him slither
through caked makeup. I could hear
spring skidding towards summer,
that deep heat we worshipped and feared.
Who knew where any of us would be in a year?
Pot smoke rose and clouded our windows. I chose
a college whose mascot was extinct.

Masters of the Universe

I need to clock someone,
split skin, but the evening is being
so goddamn agreeable, the city
like a sibling fixing my flat.
So instead I buy socks, jeans tight
enough to chafe my thighs.
Wasn't I the kid who was always
fine, content with whichever
slice was mine? While classmates
crushed insects and busted lips,
my battles raged plastic
action-figures — break a limb
and they still wouldn't blink.
I didn't think I needed vengeance,
not when Ben Dobrowski
stole my He-Man, or Peter Barkoff
called me *fag*. But now, it's as if
I never knew me. I might
be Samson, hair wild, captive
in a castle aching to snap.

Old Testament

You tell me
you are ruthless
and vengeful
as God.

Then you grab me
and kiss me
hard
on the lips.

I love God
I answer, tasting
the blood.

I say *God*
you look good
with your buttons
undone.

A Commercial Looping on Sports Radio

A guy asks a girl if she loves him.
His voice sounds young
and absurdly good-natured,
and in the background, I hear
an easy breeze, the whisk of a Frisbee
slicing the near-distance.
It's a soundscape to soothe, a track
I'd use to lull the kids to sleep.
A guy asks a girl if she loves him,
yet when the girl chirps, *Sure,*
as if offered a breath mint,
even the static stills and I think,
Abort. Run for your life!
like that night in high school
when I gave no warning,
lurched forward, landed my lips
on Jenna Lapkin's nose.
No driveway or highway or island
felt long enough to escape
my own idiocy, that small buzz-
saw grating against my brain.
But this guy digs in, scrapes a layer
of muck off his marketable heart
and asks, *Do you love me*
more than the new iced blueberry
latte from Dunkin? I picture
a Sunday in Bryant Park.
An engagement ring burning a hole
in his cargos. Two frothy beverages
sweating in the grass. *Well...*
the girl starts, then spills
into laughter, and we're left
with a voice-over imploring us
to act fast. These days, each kiss
is expected. I don't
even think. I close my eyes.

First Born

Your love for me lies between
a toy zebra and the separation of light

and darkness on the wall.
The zebra smiles, spins in your sight-

line. Blue and pink ringlets fall
from each hoof. Shadows weave

loose-limbed through the living room.
My clownish singing can't win

your glance. But at night, I watch your ghost
in the baby monitor: your moon

face, cocoon of fleece. I guess
you'll be waking soon. Just say when.

Playground

Now that I'm a father, I am here
all the time playing hide-
and-seek, coaxing my daughter
down a four-foot slide.

I've become familiar
with rubber mulch flooring,
those pigeon-splattered
benches where beat, adoring

parents blink into their phones.
How I have grown
to admire the mindful
older child, the ball thrown

back and forth again.
My daughter has her friends
and I have mine,
a kind, grey-flecked band

of thirty-somethings who knew
this was coming, but didn't think
it was coming so soon.
Lives enlarged, our victories slink

through juice box straws:
the tantrum skipped,
that girl who claws
all the other girls shipped

away on vacation. Still,
you'd guess this was paradise
the way we race and giggle,
then launch our children into the skies.

In Praise of Trains

All the best stories are indebted to trains,
each with its window seat
of classic steam, shattered lovers
abstracted by rain. The coats and hats

smack of autumn. Tongues like trout
frozen in a crate. Last night, I saw a man
dance at the carnival and could not imagine
what he looked like standing still.

Hear the pistons. Smell the wet wool.
See a single beige suitcase, barely filled,
as though she were leaving
for only the weekend.

Letters to the Dead

You get buried and away
with anything. You stand us up
at dinner, strand us at the altar,
leave us doing damage-
control for birthdays missed,
meetings not met. Years pass
and you're still deceased,
still not spilling your minestrone recipe
or that card trick you learned
in Peru. Dear dead, do you suffer?
Does emptiness get old
or do you just grow into it?
Last night, I saw you in the zoo
of my dreams, a dull-eyed tiger
pacing a cage. Tell me, do you miss it?
Do you miss lips, the sum
of a tongue, dumb questions
and witty quips? If I never wrote
you, would we ever speak?

2.

The Past

So much is known. And so little. And so
goes the blur that were your parents young
like grainy footage of grains of sand:
your father behind the camcorder, his jokes
and dark eyes. Your mother in a sunhat, pointing
towards the sea. Then comes the everyday
joys and follies, routines and degrees.
Each fact a guise, a best guess, a wild goose
you let go, because who the hell domesticates
geese? You appear half-formed, a sketch
on the streets of Long Beach or Burlington,
not to mention one heat-streaked summer in Salemi
in that Grecian sandpit spitting up fragments,
where *The Past* was everywhere, and rising
from the earth as bowl-shard and bone,
only it wasn't *yours*, or yours alone, though
with each troweled stroke, or excavated grove,
or scooped-out dawn you were making it so.

Tereska

Tereska grew up in a German concentration camp...
Asked to depict 'home' on the blackboard, she drew
only confusing lines.

—Tom Beck
(photograph by David Seymour, 1948)

In Seymour's postwar photo of her,
Tereska's face is not the face
of a child, but a tiny raccoon caged
in daylight, fleeced of ease.
Still, her picture of *home* seems
accurate enough: manic, ceaseless
barracks of chalk, barbed coils
twisting in infinity, a black-
board of nowhere. What exactly
did the doctors expect her to draw?
In her split brow and tight jaw,
I imagine my grandmother,
a survivor who never uttered
a word on the subject, and wonder
what *home* looked like to her.
Did a husband, two children, a patio
overlooking a crush of petunias
finally make sense of that term,
or did it spiral inside her, worm
behind eyelids like the stark,
guarded glare of Tereska,
drawn forever from both her task
and the camera; caught
between worlds, committed
to neither. But taken, I turn back,
struck by the sheer intensity
of her stare. Is something there
over Seymour's left shoulder,
just beyond the reach of our seeing?
Did she notice a sparrow,
a shiver of light? Did it shadow
the doorway like a father's coat?

Father of Daughters

I always figured I'd be the father
of daughters the way a zebra imagines

he must one day be a meal
of pulpy purple meat, ribcage

picked clean, and so prepares himself
on the great, grassy plains

where rubber-necked vultures
practice disinterest, and lions wait

for a break in formation,
though most days sink into pink

horizons, and are warm and fine
but for the priming of his heart. I always

figured I'd be the father of daughters,
and now that I am, I am torn apart.

Apart

It begins small:
a call unanswered.
Dinner plans postponed.
Your brother's birthday
came and went.
You turn in
one night without
brushing your teeth
and dream like a window
the instant before
it breaks. You wake
and it is broken.
You go back to sleep.

Guilt
(for my mother)

Your brother got hitched to a shiksa
in Michigan, and there you were
in Mexico City,
crazy for a Catholic boy
willing to convert. It was 1973.
You knew guilt. The dead
weight of being raised
by survivors, and a past so close
you could taste it
in the soup, in each piece
of noodle pudding placed
on your plate.
No wonder you needed
his hands on your shoulders,
the scent of fresh produce
sizzling in a pan.
Last summer, you showed me
his picture: a handsome man posing
in a garden. The grainy light
of late afternoon.
You'd been fighting
with Dad again, some typical
disaster, and I remember thinking,
You should've married that guy
in the garden. And Dad, a good man
you simply can't stand,
I'm sure he too
might have been with another
if not for some shame, some luck.

Luck

Since I am an accident, a spare
      seed, sperm t-boned

      into a sleepy ravine, I crane
my neck when metal collides.

Rear-ended fenders look
      like luck, for what but luck

      keeps skulls unscathed, glass
unsmashed? Name a place

more dependent on strangers
      to remain sober, stay awake.

      Maybe it's the sirens' candy-
apple wail, a woman in blue

laying flares like a séance,
      or the sudden ejection, bodies

      thrown clear that hold
my glance: slick road, patch

of black ice. A god who'd keep us,
      then leave us to chance.

First Mercy

What mercy is there
if while feeding the baby,

what slips down her wind-
pipe will not rise?

And what diction exists
for how lips part,

a mid-syllable
tilted over the sink?

Terror, it turns out,
is immense in its stillness.

Pitiless as newsprint
in a language

you can't speak,
it does not even

not care, but settles in
amid the stainless

steel cookware
and dried out bonsai

browning in its bowl.
It clings to curtains,

to that dull landscape
framed across the hall

until you dig your finger
in and evict it.

Relief is a rush
of oxygen. I swear

you'll shudder
when it opens the door.

Playing Airplane with my Niece

I don't notice the ceiling fan
until it nearly scalps her,
her small head lifted
towards the void, my small life
shuddering at the whip.
But that's it. No one sees
or cares, and my niece
even begs me, *Again, again!*
To hoist her into that spinning
thing, until I wonder
if it wasn't so awful after all,
so near, the way horror
can seem subject to the convenience
of our reactions, a question
of taste. Or how we all sit down
for bagels and cream cheese
while a blinkless whitefish
lies gutted and agape.

The Man on Fire
(Kaufman Studios Fair — Astoria, NY)

The man on fire is trained not to burn
but to look like he is burning.
Behind him, a woman cascades
off a crane, and at noon, a squad-car
will slam through a barn,
but the man on fire is trained not to burn.
He wears dark clothes, gloves, and a ski-mask.
He places a utility grill lighter to his wrist.
The man on fire becomes the man
on fire as it leaps up his elbow,
his torso, his back. A show-dog, it obeys
him, hurdles and begs. Rolls
and plays dead. Past the cones,
people snap photos of the man on fire.
An artificial snow-maker blows
artificial snow. But the man knows
his gig is short-lived. Soon, even his salves
and fire-resistant fabrics will give,
for while the man on fire is trained not
to burn, his training is no match
for what writhes upon him, this rising
towards ash, a heat-cloak roped
over countless centuries, cities and bodies,
and so the man must signal for his team
to step in before flames recall
what they are and become him.

Bombshell

Ever this hunger. You can lose a finger
     pointing out the moon, its white mouth

     widened in prayer. Or our neighbors upstairs,
all clamor and bedsprings, appetite bleated

into each heated beat. Please help
     yourself to seconds. Forgive us this mess.

     Till dawn, a chorus conceived against sleep:
squeak — squeak — squeak — squeak...

The Lives of Ex-Girlfriends

This sudden love
of apricots.
Is it wrong to long
for every one,

to wonder who wed,
which t-shirts each kept?
Soon your wife
will return

from work, shed her day
to a corner hamper,
but for now
you remember

walks across campus,
sweet promises
in dark bars.
How mouths kiss

with the smack
of addicts.
A fruit so delicious
you don't notice its pit.

The Apple and the World

A bearded man offers you an apple
in an alley, no less,
on your walk home from work.
An apple, you think,
are you fucking kidding?
You tell your wife about this,
the apple and the world
gone awry, the way
the man lurched, like a troll
as you passed. You say,
I swear the guy was gonna stuff me
in his backpack. You say,
I'll buy my own produce, thank you
very much. You say,
what's next, a boiling potion?
An ominous well?
But your wife isn't listening.
She is growing wings.

Infidelis

Turned on by house
fires, the howl of sirens

too far off. We grow restless
in the soapy trance

of contentment: each
darkened match, the arc

of a swing. It slips in
between sound decisions,

our *Tempur-Pedics*
and baby-proofed homes.

It shows up tipsy
when we are certain

it has split. Bolt the door.
Draw the curtains.

Forgive us our sins
we will never commit.

Schoolyard with the United States Painted on Asphalt

Whoever designed this,
separating states
into blue, yellow, pine-green
decided to divide us
with a volleyball net:
a taut incision
clear across Kansas,
North and South
at it again.
He or she fixed
this metaphor
upon a city schoolyard
where a weary boy weeps
over Jersey,
his elbow skinned
in Pittsburgh.
Whoever did this
is in some way responsible
for the troubles
of our land, the battle
breaking out between Texas
and Louisiana,
where two children
yell *Mine!,* bodies collide,
and a lost globe
plunges into the Gulf.

What Drowning Is

We know better
than to flip

our raft:
the roaring

white water
more brackish green,

each cheap oar
a sort of forced

handshake. We
know better,

but the world,
we believe, has a habit

of protecting us,
pressing pause

just before the blade
sinks in.

      *

Stacking
kickboards

into cubbies,
you told me

your counselor
touched you there.

We were eleven,
and so I laughed,

and so you laughed,
but later,

playing ping-pong
by the lake,

I eased my backhand,
fed you lobs,

took topspin
off my serve.

     *

We think we get
what drowning is,

that gasp
and shimmer

seen on TV,
something to stun

the others on land.
We know

better, yet when
the rapids

lean in, all heavy
and seething,

we tilt with them,
and our boat

plummets, quiet
in the sprays.

*

You left your flashlight,
half your clothes,

a motorized fan, a can
of soda. You left

your comic books
and ping-pong paddle.

Kept your sketch pad.
Kept your cleats.

You left on a Monday
in your parents' minivan,

while our camp director
smiled and sighed

and hugged his chest,
then sent us out

to play dodgeball
until dinner.

*

We fold bow-first, roll
and keep rolling,

smacking one another
in the mouths

with our oars.
We do not know

this panic
between our ribs,

what wild indifference
pins us below.

Our deaths
smell of smoke

and soaked granola.
Or wait—

that's the scent
of everything coming to.

First Wish

I watch my daughter
drop a penny

into the fountain,
stand there

a minute, then pick
it back out.

Paris Pastoral

You wore that yellow flower top
the whole trip.
Your father's leather belt.
Had you toppled into blossoms,
I'd have lost you forever.
Museums? Monuments? We forgot
it was holiday — Easter break —
each holy cathedral packed
with khakis and sandals, tourists
at the oiled throat of art.
Knowing nothing so shameful
as Americans acting American
in Europe, we groped
our days from dive bar
to wine bar, swigging cheap reds
we couldn't afford.
I remember one bookstore.
The arc of a bridge. A man took
our picture at Sacré Coeur,
and as payment, tried kissing
the inside of your wrist.

Berlin, etc.

Before the war, there was war
on architecture. On art. Think mink
nightlife stifled by gunfire,
the picked clean witness
of galleries, books in the heap.
      Beneath our feet,
solid sediments soiled by bone,
smoothed over, the unmarked bunker
headstoned by condos.
The white sky is about face.
Our bald tour-guide skips
the serious bits, brags about breweries
and Thai food by the Wall.
      Maybe I'm old
fashioned, but I keep expecting the snap-
back of a burlap sack over my head,
a roundup of us stragglers.
Yet here I am, snapping selfies
with municipal buildings, a column
of Victory; that golden lady
up there, ready to leap.

Frogs
(Natural History Museum)

Since all I recall of eighth-grade Biology
      is the fleshy balloon of Mr. Manfree's face,
and the gelatinous, white-bellied bodies

      we divided, I take my family to see the frogs:
brilliant, lethal, like tiny jewels with toxins
      in their skin. We pay the suggested donation

to watch them watch us, warily, (they are
      endangered after all,) each thin-lidded eyeball
as if wise to what slop we made of their

      relatives: mini-massacres on disinfected trays.
But these stay whole — poised moisture –
      their controlled enclosures humming with prey.

Then a quick flick, pink tongue-projectile
      so sudden and brutal and thoroughly casual,
we find ourselves armed with nothing but praise.

Fall Praise

      The seasons save us from hating ourselves.
The keys in my pocket might as well

          be a knife. At the park, we wheel solar-
protected strollers while lean teenagers

      ollie off guardrails, tag benches with illegible loops,
slip cigarettes between newly kissed lips.

          Praise be the joggers with their scissored precision,
      the pigeon lady with suspicions

of the moon. It *is* getting late. The light redistributing.
      Our community pool closed till spring.

3.

Driving the Wrong Way Down a One-Way Street

For an instant, you're the last sane person
on earth. The windows are down.
TD Bank glows like a green mausoleum.
There's sunlight in the branches, and a voice

on the radio talking last night's debate.
Who won? Will it translate in the polls?
You're only half-listening, dreaming
about *Homeland* once the kids go to bed.

Still, there are signs: a woman with a backpack
stiffens mid-step. Each parked car glowers
its wide, glassy eye. You grip the wheel,
but feel nothing for the road that empties

beneath you, the early-autumn wind
with its childish tug. Something is up ahead,
moving closer and closer. It's become clear
you have no idea where you live.

— *10/11/16*

You Want It Darker

The day after the election, Leonard Cohen dies
and my eye gets infected, and my daughter
flies around the living room refusing to put on underwear.
I can barely lift my head to see the smug sun
pouring through the blinds, streaming its white spotlight
on each darkened wall. I'm all in on grief and misery.
All in shock and *Fuck this Country*, but it's still a day, a day
I don't teach, but strap my son into his Cheerio-
encrusted stroller and wheel him to his 'baby-taps'
dance class at the Y. We arrive to find the teacher red-eyed
and wrecked, her t-shirt wrinkled, acoustic slung low.
Only one other parent has bothered to show,
her kid wailing beneath the moon-glow of her phone.
When it becomes clear no one else is coming,
the teacher begins to strum and sing of fall, of piggies
at market and monkeys in our beds. We squeeze
our fingers into spinning fists and imagine
we are busses peeling out of town. It all culminates
in the world's saddest rendition of "If you're happy
and you know it," in which we're summoned to rise up
off our multi-colored mats, to clap and stomp
and shout, *Hooray!* — Oh, God. Oh, Leonard,
who shed this life like a pinstripe suit, who saw this mess
and chose not to stay, but slip between the bricks
in his Tower of Song, the sun is still out there,
armored and gleaming. There is nothing I can say
to make it stop.

"What to Do in Duanesburg, NY"

Not a thing, according to
the completely blank,
though prominently displayed
tack-board in town.

It stands before us, a pool
of framed beige,
a wasteland of old pinholes
and small-town potential.

Where is the farmers' market?
Their trivia night?
Why no fliers
for some aged, acoustic duo

armed with James Taylor
and Donovan covers?
On this cold November evening,
it makes us chuckle

the way honesty can
when it comes
out of nowhere—the quick,
electric surge of it

like cables sparking life
to a pickup out back.

To Swim in a Lake in Which Someone Has Drowned

is to offer fate its victory lap: limp wrists,
        a dangling ankle. It is to think of search boats

        skimming still waters, the black hair of netting
knotted with kelp. To swim in a lake

in which someone has drowned is to know
        this world will kill us if we let it, the balmiest

        Tuesday looking for an excuse. Must we forgive
each ripple? Every swell and current? Pull

anchors from our aching limbs? My love, can you
        feel it, this sinking as we swim?

Changing the Subject

In the kitchen, with the kids finally asleep,
and news of another shooting
in the space between us,
you confess you think death
might feel like giving birth, the body
insistent, having its way.
You say you'd never been so at the mercy
of yourself as you were on that bed,
in that cloud-thin gown, and just the knowing
it was coming: ruthless
transformation.
        I have no good response
to *ruthless transformation*, and so it hangs there
beside a bowl of old tortilla chips
and black-bean salsa
we've decided will be dinner. It lingers
while a reporter frames chaos
as *developments*; her shoulders rinsed in darkness
and revolving red lights. I want
to kiss you. Build asylum inside you.
Let our bodies change
        the subject, the channel
to cartoons. Before night pulls away
down the flickering interstate,
I want one ruined thing utterly redeemed: a death-
toll rescinded, a swastika removed,
my uncle's melanoma caught early enough
to be a chat, a beige Band-Aid
halfway down his calf. *It had looked*,
my aunt said, *like little more*
than an ink-spot. I didn't get nervous
till it didn't wash out.

First Mark

She bursts in with slashes
and swirls, tiny fingers

so furiously stained that I picture
the nubby remains

of crayons, her makeshift table
more chaotic than mine,

and I fear for her life, this little life
that must be persuaded

not to swallow glass, or dash
in front of trucks, though I admire

the plain intensity of her work,
each mark a crimson play

at permanence, a claim upon the page,
and so I ask her to explain

this bloody offering, to tell me
what it is we have made.

Numbers

My grandmother never trusted calculators,
but crunched numbers in a spiral notebook
at the kitchen table, watching her news.
Work harder so I'll have more to count,
she'd snap at my father, so he worked
harder, fixed more mufflers, stapled receipts,
but the numbers didn't change. Grandma barked,
No more garbage! though our house gleamed,
bone-dry. Only after she died did my parents
discover how much she had saved us—
banked in binders, vaulted in bonds, solid blue
digits crowding each page. She left them
in the kitchen by her black-and-white television
we tossed a week later, though it worked fine.

First Answer

My daughter wants to know
when I became

a grown-up. I tell her

I became one
the day you were born.

Spoils

When my four-year-old shoves
a toy block in my face
and screams, *Cheeeeese!*
I realize there is spoil
in all preservation,
in the quick clicks of keeping
intact, and I see how
reasonable it is to believe
each photo steals a sliver of soul,
if you believe in souls,
which I do or don't
depending on how poorly
the children nap, on the way dawn
frames their features,
the zoom-resolution, my view
of the world. Is it me,
or do I already owe them
an apology for every time I step out
of myself, detach mid-
snack, story or recital,
only to return with moonlight
between my teeth, some
sudden articulation. And is it wrong
to articulate this, to speak
of them now as props
in a poem, a pose held longer
than anyone should bear?

Answering Machine, 2003
(for Nate)

Two weeks after you found your mother
dead in her bedroom, heart given out,

I called and heard her tell me she was gone,
to leave a message, have a nice day.

I rang again, thinking pizza, anything
to pull you from that house so entirely *hers*,

off the sofa she picked, eating Pop-Tarts
she bought. But you never picked up,

your mom did, and she'd sound no
different than when asking about school,

or if I was staying late, what we felt like
for dinner. She sounded no different.

Now it's been years and I only hear you
in echoes, ghost-speak, our cord

cut, but Nate, this is me trying to call
and say what goes without saying.

Meditation in the Key of an Exhale

It's my party and I'll cry if I want to,
says my son at his bris, though it's my party
and I carry the weight of a hundred generations
on the tip of my penis might be more apt.
Or: It's my party. Let us pray. The truth is
it isn't a party (in my family) until somebody cries
or storms off in shame, barricading themselves
in the opposite-sex restroom, while my son,
for what it's worth, hardly cried at all
at the critical juncture, just sucked the wine-
soaked rag between his gums the way Abraham
bit the branch of a thick-knuckled olive tree
when he snipped himself, joining a club
he was the sole member of. Party
of one. *Is it still my party?* asks my son slumped
in the pocket of my elbow. He looks just
like his sonogram ghost on the fridge:
my lips, my wife's nose, and who knows
whose chin. It's my poetry and I promise not to cry
when I read this to him, how the instant
I saw him I thought he was dead, a silence
so wide I stage-dived into it. Was it the winter
in his eyes? That umbilical noose so close
to his neck? It's my party and I predicted
a smaller turnout, less guests. I expected to be alone.
But here he is, plump as a blood plum, a part
of it now, somehow, my son, so when
the ceremony is over, and everyone is gone,
I snap him into the car seat, tighten the straps
and holy hell, my heart is in my throat.

Exodus Days

As a kid, I was schooled in guilt
and persistence, and loved
the story of how Moses lost his shit
in waves of desert, that never-

ending nothing, luckless invalids
he was delivered to lead.
I can picture them bickering,
some hotshot insisting

he knew the way. When my days
go south, the sky a damp rag
twisting above me, I think of Moses
with his stick and lisp, a plague

of locusts humming in his eyelids,
dried lamb's blood tinting each fist. Yes,
I can imagine a man splitting sea,
then regretting it instantly.

Self-Portrait with Gravity

The day before I dove off an airplane,
a hang-glider struck the same green field,
hit the earth like it wanted to hurt it.
The Swede said he'd heard from the hostel,
how nothing was wrong until everything was:
cables stripped of rubber casings.
A neon wing pinned in salute. You could still
see the divot, that bruise of dirt
where limbs had splintered, yet there I was
in goggles and jumpsuit, knowing only
I didn't want my parents to know.
And so I boarded the plane, paid in full
before leaving the ground. Against good sense,
I looked down before jumping, but all I saw
softened with distance as I felt how
the pastures might catch me when I fell.

The Grounds

Step into this
and reach nowhere
forever: just acres

of grass and absence
and sky, here
you'll learn to live

with yourself
swallow your echo
bury your goals

surely you can stay
become part
of the grounds

an occasional yellow sign
alerting visitors
of your crossing.

The Process

Crazy that at twenty
I thought I was old. I'd slide
my past into plastic sleeves
and call it *The Past*
and somehow believe
I was no longer in it.
I would walk the streets—
a college sophomore stubborn
with kindness—picking
splinters from my shadow.
Trying to unify the sovereign
islands of my beard.
Now what I fear
is how little slips away,
how life trails me
like a massive tail smacking
everything I pass.
How one day, I'll look back
to find display cases
shattered, aisles
destroyed, polite smiles
of the recently thwacked.
That was me? I'll be asking,
guilty or impressed
before I bolt for the exit,
or pay what I owe.

Upon Hearing That Someone Has Forgotten Their Laptop, iPhone, Keys, Wallet and Dog Leash at Airport Security

I remember in fifth-grade
losing two jackets
in two days. Both times it was snowing,
and my parents, more concerned
than ticked off, kept asking,
But didn't you feel the wind?
I confess now I felt something wind-ish,
some dull vacancy
tugging my bones. That must be
what this person feels,
his belongings
droning over the Terminal D intercom,
a plastic bin of himself
like bacteria in a Petri dish.
I crane my neck, half-expecting
to spot this traveler
smiling past snow globes
and duty-free booze,
or sprinting after his beloved
schnauzer. Either way, I wish him well.
Haven't we all been there — not all there — before:
hustling to keep up, make
connections, leaving so many
essentials behind.

Training

For our son will not sleep,
or immediately snaps awake
without song + steady pat
upon his back, we must make him
wail the wail of the forsaken.
At our pediatrician's strict instructions,
we must stop picking him up.
Shut the door. We must make him wail
the wail of the forsaken.
Though his stunned face may break
into howling, his mouth
a tiny cavern of despair, we must
betray him. We must train
our hearts for the marathon ahead.
We must fashion a solid muscle
of our love and make him
wail the wail of the forsaken.
There are so many ways to be cruel
in this world, small takings
that giveth none. I just want our son
to go to bed, but he pulls up
on the crib in his banana-print pajamas,
demanding answers, demanding
a hug. *Must you make me*
wail the wail of the forsaken?
I try to explain our predicament to him
through a wall which separates
his bedroom from ours. I try
not to hear the wails of the forsaken,
though his tears are real,
and each wail is holy in its appeal
for affection; this bone-pierced prayer
he must answer alone.

Driving Through a Blizzard

I saw my own death
        through a squint of windshield,
in each bleached guardrail, echo

        of road. Even my heart
was a heap of metal until flawless as fists
        driven though drywall,

two giant bulls lunged
        into vision. Their massive skulls
collided like boulders,

        hooked horns blaring attack.
I slowed, sputtered, nearly spun
        out staring as their barreling bodies

erupted from white. Then suddenly,
        they were gone. And I slid, twisting
through the storm to find you.

Acknowledgements

Thank you to the editors of the following publications in which many of these poems first appeared, sometimes in different versions:

Alaska Quarterly Review: "Berlin, etc."

American Poetry Review: "Changing the Subject," "Go So You Can Come Back," "Letters to the Dead," "Local News," "The Apple and the World," "Training," "Upon Hearing That Someone Has Forgotten...," & "Veterans Day, 2014"

Arts & Letters: "A Commercial Looping on Sports Radio," "Father of Daughters," & "Spoils"

Asheville Poetry Review: "You Want It Darker"

The Brooklyn Quarterly: "Apart"

Bennington Review: "Legion" & "Playing Airplane with my Niece"

burnt district: "First Mercy"

*Carve Magazine: "*The Lives of Ex-Girlfriends"

Chicago Quarterly Review: "Fall Praise"

Cold Mountain Review: "Numbers"

Columbia Journal Online: "Old Testament"

Diode Poetry Journal: "All Possible Fates," "The Man on Fire" & "The Grounds"

EPOCH: "New View"

The Gettysburg Review: "In Praise of Trains"

Jabberwock Review: "To Swim in a Lake in Which Someone Has Drowned"

Massachusetts Review: "Meditation in the Key of an Exhale"

Mudfish: "Exodus Days"

Newtown Literary: "Bombshell"

Nice Cage: "First Mark" & "Infidelis"

The Normal School: "Driving Through a Blizzard" & "Those of Us Who Cannot Recall Our Dreams"

Poetry Ireland Review: "Masters of the Universe"

PRISM International: "Answering Machine, 2003" & "Guilt"

River Styx: "Luck"

Salamander: "Frogs"

Shenandoah: "Senior Cut Day"

The Southern Review: "My Years in Tacoma, Without Exaggeration"

Tampa Review: "Self-Portrait with Gravity"

The Threepenny Review: "Schoolyard with the United States Painted on Asphalt"

"Veterans Day, 2014" was awarded the 2015 'Stanley Kunitz Memorial Prize' from the *American Poetry Review*. "You Want It Darker" was awarded the 2017 'William Matthews Poetry Prize' from the *Asheville Poetry Review*. "Father of Daughters" & "Schoolyard with the United States Painted on Asphalt" were reprinted for *Poetry Daily*. "Numbers" was chosen by Ted Kooser for his weekly newsletter, *American Life in Poetry*. "To Swim in a Lake in Which Someone Has Drowned" was nominated for a *Pushcart Prize*.

My grateful appreciation to Queens Council on the Arts for supporting this project by awarding me an "Individual Artist Grant" in 2015.

Thank you to Patty Paine, Law Alsobrook, and everyone at Diode Editions for believing in this book and working so hard on it.

To my parents, who taught me what home is, and gave me a wonderful one. To Ilan, awesome older brother, role model and photographer extraordinaire. To Ronen, awesome younger brother and the most selfless person I know. Get rid of that jacket already! To the rest of my wonderful, crazy, loving family – thank you.

I've been very lucky to have so many incredible readers, teachers and friends. Thank you to Dan Levine, Ilan Morris, Téa Obreht and Alexi Zentner for your friendship, advice and for laughing with me along the way. Thank you to Elizabeth Schmidt, Huck Gutman, Leslie Heywood, Liz Rosenberg, Maria Mazziotti Gillan, Susan Deer Cloud, Alice Fulton, Ken McClane, Will Cordeiro, Maria Crimi, Dan Sheehan, Jon Lewis-Katz, Mark Doty, Tim Green, April Ossmann, Elizabeth Scanlon, Lee Upton, BJ Ward and my super-supportive colleagues at NCC. Thank you to Joe Pan, Wendy Pan and the BAP family. Thank you to my band-mates, past and present.

Thank you to the entire Queens literary community, which is ever-growing and beautiful. I'm especially indebted to my APC crew: Nancy Agabian, Catherine Fletcher, Mary Lannon, Meera Nair, Sokunthary Svay and Vaughn Watson. Thank you to Richard Jeffrey Newman, KC Trommer, Maria Lisella, Micah Eaton Zevin and Rosebud Ben-Oni.

To my daughter, Neta, who amazes me daily, and wrote some of the best lines in this book.

To my son, Oren, who loves basketball and cookies, hates sleeping, and is utterly delicious.

And finally, to Yael, because I love you.

Jared Harél has been awarded the 'Stanley Kunitz Memorial Prize' from *American Poetry Review*, as well as the 'William Matthews Poetry Prize' from *Asheville Poetry Review*. Additionally, his poems have appeared in such journals as the *Bennington Review, Massachusetts Review, The Southern Review*, and *Tin House*. Harél teaches writing at Nassau Community College, plays drums, and lives in Queens, NY with his wife and two kids.